The World's Deadliest

The Deadliest Jobs
on Earth

by Connie Colwell Miller

Raintree

www.raintreepublishers.co.uk
Visit our website to find out
more information about
Raintree books.

To order:
☎ Phone 0845 6044371
🖹 Fax +44 (0) 1865 312263
🖳 Email myorders@raintreepublishers.co.uk

Customers from outside the UK please telephone +44 1865 312262

Raintree is an imprint of Capstone Global Library
Limited, a company incorporated in England and
Wales having its registered office at 7 Pilgrim
Street, London, EC4V 6LB – Registered company
number: 6695582

Edited by Abby Czeskleba
Designed by Matt Bruning
Media research by Svetlana Zhurkin
Production by Laura Manthe
Originated by Capstone Global Library Ltd
Printed and bound in China by South China
Printing Company Ltd

ISBN 978 1 406 21830 5
14 13 12 11 10
10 9 8 7 6 5 4 3 2 1

**British Library Cataloguing in Publication
Data**
Miller, Connie Colwell,
The deadliest jobs on Earth. -- (The world's
deadliest)
363.1'19-dc22
A full catalogue record for this book is available
from the British Library.

Acknowledgements
We would like to thank the following for
permission to reproduce photographs:
Alamy p. **27** (Chris Cheadle); Corbis p.
7 (Arctic Images); Getty Images pp. **15**
(Bloomberg News/ Adeel Halim), **19** (Dan
Kirkwood), **29** (Reportage/Christopher Pillitz),
21, **23** (Stone/Tyler Stableford), **11** (The
Image Bank/Chip Porter); Photolibrary p. **5**
(Alaskastock); Rex Features pp. **17** (Heathcliff
O'Malley), **25** (Sinopix/ Colin Galloway);
Shutterstock pp. **28** (Andrejs Pidjass - design
element), **13** (Anthony Jay D. Villalon), **12**
(dedaiva bg, - design element), **26** (Dole -
design element); **18** (Ivan Harisovich Khafizov
- design element), **28** (objects fo rall - design
element), **16** (Richard Sargeant - design
element), **9** (Thomas Sztanek), **20** (World pics
- design element), **26** (Zsolt Horvath - design
element).

Cover photograph of a firefighter reproduced
with permission of Getty Images (Stone/ Mike
Harrington); cover design elements by Ilja
Mašík, (Shutterstock), and Yuri Bershadsky.

CONTENTS

Some words are printed in bold, **like this**. You can find out what they mean on page 30. You can also look in the box at the bottom of the page where they first appear.

DEADLY JOBS

Rough seas, raging flames, and wild weather are just a few of the dangers that workers face around the world. Every day, people **risk** injury or death in their jobs.

risk take a chance that may cause injury or death

DEADLY *FACT*

If you get hurt on a fishing boat, there is no one to drive you to hospital.

SLIGHTLY DANGEROUS

LORRY DRIVER

Lorry drivers around the world face dangers on the road. Poor weather or bad driving can cause accidents. Lorries carrying dangerous chemicals are especially at **risk**. In a crash, the lorries could explode.

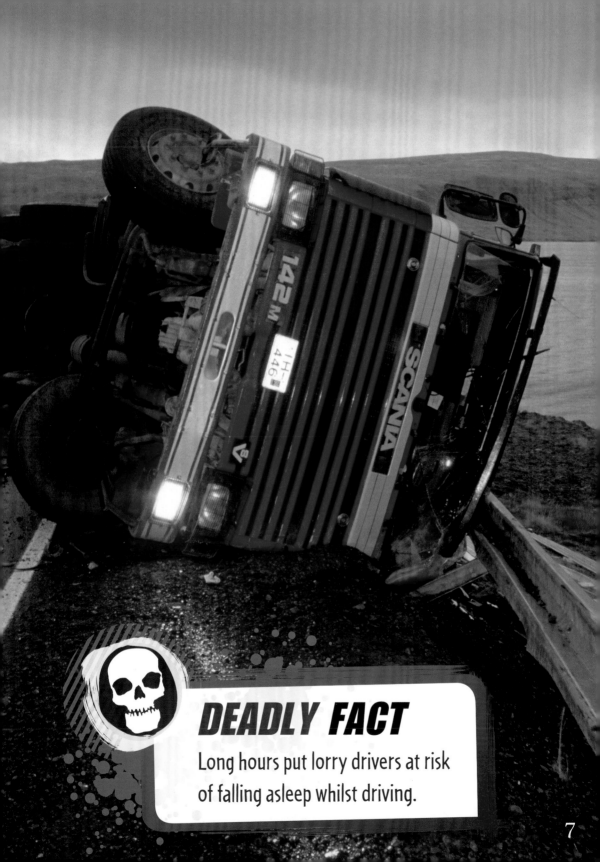

DEADLY *FACT*

Long hours put lorry drivers at risk of falling asleep whilst driving.

FEARLESS FARMERS

Farmers use powerful machines on their farms. A combine harvester uses sharp **blades** to cut the crops. Other farm machines have huge **rollers**. Farmers can get caught and injured in the machines.

blade part of a tool that has a sharp edge

roller tube-shaped object that turns and is used to flatten things

SMALL PLANE PILOT

The pilots of small planes face many dangers in the air. Storms can hit small planes or engines can fail. Flights over foggy mountains are especially dangerous and deadly.

DEADLY FACT

Rescue workers have a hard time rescuing people in the mountains.

HIGH VOLTAGE

Electrical power line workers handle dangerous wires. Workers can be burned or **electrocuted** by the large, powerful wires. They often work from great heights and **risk** deadly falls.

electrocute injure or kill by electricity

VERY DANGEROUS

DEADLY SITES

Cars and lorries whizz past roadworks at high speeds. Fast-moving vehicles can hit workers. Bulldozers, diggers, and cranes can also cause deadly injuries.

SOLDIERS

Soldiers fight in deadly battles. They can be injured whilst using heavy machinery or firing weapons. Soldiers travel in armed vehicles that can crash or be attacked.

DEADLY FACT

Over 100 British soldiers were killed in Afghanistan in 2009.

KEEPING ORDER

Police officers fight dangerous **criminals**. Some criminals carry hidden weapons. Police officers also help to keep large crowds calm at events.

DEADLY *FACT*

Police sometimes **risk** death catching criminals in high-speed car chases.

criminal someone who breaks the law

BURIED ALIVE

Miners crawl deep underground to dig up **minerals**. They spend long hours in small spaces without fresh air. Cave-ins can trap the miners underground.

mineral material found in the ground that is not an animal or a plant

DEADLY FACT

Thousands of people die each year inside coal mines.

EXTREMELY DANGEROUS

FIGHTING FIRES

Raging flames and blinding smoke put firefighters at risk. Forest fires can cause deadly burns. Firefighters can also die from breathing in too much smoke.

SCAFFOLDERS

Scaffolders fix **scaffolding** to the sides of buildings. Strong winds can blow them off the scaffolding to their deaths. Falling planks can also hit them without warning.

DEADLY FACT

People on the ground have been killed by objects falling off scaffolding. Even wheelbarrows have fallen off!

scaffolding planks and metal poles fixed together for workers to walk on

FOREST LOGGER

Loggers cut down trees with **chainsaws** and other dangerous tools. Logging is dangerous. Loggers may fall out of tall trees or be hit by falling branches.

chainsaw saw with a motor and cutting teeth on a chain that moves round

FREEZING WATERS

Deep-sea fishing is one of the world's most dangerous jobs. Fishermen can get tangled in the nets and pulled overboard. Large waves can also knock the fishermen into the freezing water.

DEADLY *FACT*

Many ships have disappeared in the Atlantic Ocean in an area called the Bermuda Triangle.

GLOSSARY

blade part of a tool that has a sharp edge

chainsaw saw with a motor that has cutting teeth on a chain that moves round

criminal someone who breaks the law

electrocute injure or kill by electricity

mineral material found in the ground that is not an animal or a plant

risk take a chance that may cause injury or death

roller tube-shaped object that turns and is used to flatten things

scaffolding planks and metal poles fixed together for workers to walk on

FIND OUT MORE

Books

The Worst Children's Jobs in History,
Tony Robinson (Macmillan, 2006)

Tough Jobs: Fighter Pilot, Helen Greathead
(A&C Black, 2008)

Websites

**http://www.yourdiscovery.com/
dangerousjobs/index.shtml**
Find out more about some of the world's
most dangerous jobs.

INDEX